INTRODUCTION

I have transitioned more times than I can remember.

From school to school, state to state, house to house, singleness to marriage, navigating transitions has become a huge part of my story.

Each transition has played a major part in cultivating my identity, my purpose, and my values I have learned so much from the seasons and situations I have walked away from and the ones I have walked into.

Some transitions have been my decision, while others were made for me. In my life, I have had to grieve people, relationships, places, positions, and patterns, all of which shaped me and had significant implications on who I am as a person.

Of course, some transitions were harder than others, but every transition has been a process. Transition is common, but I discovered that dealing with the emotion is rare. Oftentimes, we try to ignore what we feel, deny what we feel, and/or push through what we feel to the point where we do not give ourselves a chance to feel.

Some of my hardest transitions forced me to deal with my feelings, which produced this devotional. I had to study and pray myself out of some funks throughout my life. On my journey to self-discovery, I found some valuable truths worth sharing. As we aim to trust God during times of transition throughout these next 14 days, it is my goal to help every reader embrace transition when it's truly time for it and manage transition properly while in it.

Managing transitions properly takes full trust in God, but it also takes awareness and a willingness to embrace and endure your feelings. As raw as those feelings may be, they are real feelings that deserve your attention. The feelings of frustration, uncertainty, grief, rejection, fear of starting over, and more that transition can bring are all valid. These 14 days will address them, attack them head-on, and allow you to feel what you feel with a sense of great expectancy for what's to come.

Listen, I will not lie to you. Transitions can be hard. However, you do not have to transition without help. This devotional is everything I have had to process within a few pages. Throughout 14 days, I believe we can manage our transitions better while building or rebuilding our trust in God's intentions and plans for our lives despite the transition we may be facing.

Let's transition better, together.

DAY 1
TRANSITION DEFINED

Transition happens. It's inevitable.

As human beings, we face change more than we realize. There are always seasons of growth, out-growth, exits, and entrances, whether professionally, relationally, mentally, physically, emotionally, or spiritually. Transition just happens.

Simply put, transitioning is changing from one state or condition to another.

We change constantly from the day we're born to the day we leave this Earth. Whether we know it or not, we change every year. We change after every season, after every relationship, and after certain conversations. We change constantly. When we're young, change is easy. When we're older, change becomes more difficult. Nevertheless, whether we desire it or not, change happens.

And after discovering all of that, here is the crazy part. As human beings, we change constantly, but as Christians, we change even more. God gifts us opportunities to grow and evolve daily. He frequently challenges us to become better and guides us to better more often than we think. Changes for a Christian can be birthed from sermons, prayers, scriptures, conversations, songs, visions, discerning moments, and the list goes on. Change is readily available for Christians because God is waiting for us to receive better from Him.

Although all of that sounds great, the truth is that change is scary, intimidating, and disruptive; most times, it's not asked for, nor is it welcomed when it arrives. Hear me out though. Give me 14 days to make my case. I believe that although change can be uncomfortable, scary, and overwhelming, we must remember that God's intentions are for our good, even when it doesn't make sense.

You may be in the midst of a transition right now, but it doesn't have to be bad. Transition is a vehicle that transports us from one perspective to another, one door to another, one connection to another, and one opportunity to another. And guess what? Our Father is behind the wheel.

When transition is embraced, it can be a beautiful thing. So hop in and enjoy the ride.

Deuteronomy 31:8 ERV
"8 The Lord will lead you. He himself is with you. He will not fail you or leave you. Don't worry. Don't be afraid!"

Isaiah 41:13 ERV
"13 I am the Lord your God, who holds your right hand. And I tell you, 'Don't be afraid! I will help you.'

NOTES

NOTES

DAY 2
DIRECTION OR DISTRACTION

God doesn't initiate all transitions.

Most of us have multiple voices that speak to our hearts, but some only experience three: God, the enemy, and ourselves. God speaks to our hearts through the Holy Spirit, guiding us toward a better life and His destiny for our lives, while the enemy speaks to our hearts, guiding us toward fear and destruction. But most commonly, we speak to our own hearts, deciding whether to build ourselves up or to tear ourselves down.

In moments where we are navigating transition, we have to decide which voice is worth listening to. Discerning whether you've received direction from God or a distraction from the enemy involves deep reflection, prayer, and spiritual guidance. You must determine if what's spoken to your heart aligns with your values, scriptures, and the divine principles of love, peace, and goodness. Or is what's spoken to your heart in alignment with defeat, fear, or the destructive principles of ego, narcissism, and glory for yourself?

Although change happens frequently and transition is inevitable, it's important to know that God doesn't initiate all transitions. Sometimes, we end and start seasons because God instructed us to do so. Sometimes, we end seasons and start seasons because the enemy told us to. Before transition is made, we have to detect who the initiator is. Is it God? Is it the enemy? Or is it me? We must discern this transition's overall impact on us and others.

Every transition costs you something, whether it is money, time, friendships, positions, energy, etc. It is going to cost you something. However, I have noticed in my own life that transitions not initiated by God tend to cost me more. Transitions initiated by me and/or the enemy have cost me peace, joy, strength, direction, and vision, in addition to money, time, friendships, positions, and energy.

If we transition without determining the source of our transition, we run the risk of experiencing pain we are not prepared for, seeing fruit we did not plant, and living a life God did not intend. Is this pressure to change direction from God, a distraction from the enemy, or a decision you've made yourself?

1 John 4:1 ERV
"1 My dear friends, many false prophets are in the world now. So don't believe every spirit, but test the spirits to see if they are from God."

John 10:1-5 ERV
"10 Jesus said, "It is certainly true that when a man enters the sheep pen, he should use the gate. If he climbs in some other way, he is a robber. He is trying to steal the sheep. 2 But the man who takes care of the sheep enters through the gate. He is the shepherd. 3 The man who guards the gate opens the gate for the shepherd. And the sheep listen to the voice of the shepherd. He calls his own sheep, using their names, and he leads them out. 4 He brings all of his sheep out. Then he goes ahead of them and leads them. The sheep follow him, because they know his voice. 5 But sheep will never follow someone they don't know. They will run away from him, because they don't know his voice.""

Isaiah 30:21 ERV
"21 If you wander from the right path, either to the right or to the left, you will hear a voice behind you saying, "You should go this way. Here is the right way.""

NOTES

NOTES

DAY 3
YOU HAVE A CHOICE

Transition is a choice.

Most of us long for stability. It is natural to desire to settle in, even if we walk in knowing this is just for a set time. We'll say we are just taking this position to move up the ladder or we're giving this position 3-5 years and then moving on to something else. Then we look up 10 years later in the same position and on the same step of the ladder we were trying to climb. Because of our natural desire for stability, we allow ourselves to get stuck in situations, careers, relationships, mindsets, and so much more. After all, being stuck is safer than changing, right?

Temporary sometimes has a way of appearing permanent, especially if it feels good enough. We sometimes feel like we don't deserve better, so we settle into the temporary because good enough seems good enough for us. We must be careful not to allow settling-in to become settling. Transition doesn't always mean your current state is bad, but it may not be the best.

Typically, transition begins with a realization that better is possible. It starts with a reminder of your purpose, potential, or passion. You'll begin to feel like something is missing. You'll discover a lack of fulfillment. You'll begin to feel a sense of frustration. And when these feelings are felt, transition is available. Notice the word "available" though. At the end of the day, transition is still a choice you have to make. Even when God gives commands, we still have a choice. He created us to be His representatives, not His robots.

If you choose to stay put (and you can choose to stay put), those feelings of frustration and lack of fulfillment will eventually fade out, but I can not guarantee that they will never fade back in. If you choose to transition, there will be some uncertainty. But amid uncertainty, focus on what's certain: God will never leave or forsake you.

Philippians 1:6 ERV
"6 I am sure that the good work God began in you will continue until he completes it on the day when Jesus Christ comes again."

Ephesians 5:15-17 ERV
"15 So be very careful how you live. Live wisely, not like fools. 16 I mean that you should use every opportunity you have for doing good because these are evil times. 17 So don't be foolish with your lives, but learn what the Lord wants you to do."

NOTES

NOTES

DAY 4
TRUSTING GOD'S NO

God gives short answers and requires us to trust Him the rest of the way.

Transition can be challenging, especially when our will and God's will do not quite align. No's from God can shake us to our core, whether He's saying, "No, we cannot stay in what we want to stay in," or saying, "No, we cannot leave what we're trying to escape." When we receive a no from God, we have to remember His ways are not our ways, and His thoughts are above our thoughts.

We must remember that God is all-knowing even when He isn't all-sharing. He does not share all of His plans with us. He oftentimes gives short answers and requires us to trust Him the rest of the way.

- In Genesis 12:1 The Lord said to Abram, *"Leave your country and your people. Leave your father's family and go to the country that I will show you."* What kind of direction is that? At least tell me where I'm going.
- In Exodus 3, when God called Moses to stand up to Pharoah, Moses asked the question, *"But if I go to the Israelites and say to them, 'The God of your ancestors sent me,' then the people will ask, 'What is his name?' What should I tell them?"* Then God said to Moses, *"Tell them, 'I Am Who I Am.' When you go to the Israelites, tell them, 'I Am' sent me to you."* Huh God? What does that even mean?
- In the Garden of Gethsemane, Jesus begged and pleaded that God would spare Him from His assignment. *"Father, if you are willing, please don't make me drink from this cup. But do what you want, not what I want."* God didn't even respond, and Jesus had to fulfill the assignment He tried to escape.

Can you trust God even when His answers are short? Can you trust Him even if His will seems contradictory to your logic? Can you trust God even if His answer is no when all you wanted was a yes? If you're going to trust Him through this transition, it means you will have to trust Him when things seem confusing, chaotic, and contradictory.

Psalm 115:3 ERV
"3 Our God is in heaven, and he does whatever he wants."

2 Corinthians 12:7-10 ERV
"7 But I must not be too proud of the wonderful things that were shown to me. So a painful problem was given to me—an angel from Satan, sent to make me suffer so that I would not think that I am better than anyone else. 8 I begged the Lord three times to take this problem away from me. 9 But the Lord said, "My grace is all you need. Only when you are weak can everything be done completely by my power." So I will gladly boast about my weaknesses. Then Christ's power can stay in me. 10 Yes, I am glad to have weaknesses if they are for Christ. I am glad to be insulted and have hard times. I am glad when I am persecuted and have problems because it is when I am weak that I am really strong."

NOTES

NOTES

DAY 5
TRUSTING GOD'S YES

Our biggest struggles arises when we have to trust God.

We've all struggled or will sometimes struggle with receiving a no from God. In most cases, His no is a hard pill to swallow, but don't get it twisted; God's yes is not always a cakewalk. A yes from God can bring about just as much stress, anxiety, pressure, uncertainty, and worry as His no can, especially when His yes comes out of nowhere, does not match what we envisioned, or comes with more weight and burdens than anticipated. A yes from God is almost always desired, but that does not mean it is always easy.

Trusting God's yes typically requires three things:
1. A Foundation of Trust
2. An Understanding of His Will
3. A Memory of His Faithfulness

At your core, you have to believe that God wants what's best for you. In your heart, you must believe He won't lead you somewhere He can't keep you. The reality is we easily put our trust in so many things. We trust that chairs will hold us when we sit down and that cars will drive us when we crank them up. We trust that microwaves will heat our food and refrigerators will chill our food. We trust that buildings won't collapse and Google will give us the correct information. We trust the weather channel, navigation systems, pilots we don't know, and more. The biggest area where we struggle with our trust is when we have to trust God.

But when we understand that God's intention for us is good, and when we take the time to remember that all He has been to us is good, trust becomes easier.

Proverbs 3:5-6 ERV
"5 Trust the Lord completely, and don't depend on your own knowledge. 6 With every step you take, think about what he wants, and he will help you go the right way."

Jeremiah 29:11 ERV
"11 I say this because I know the plans that I have for you." This message is from the Lord. "I have good plans for you. I don't plan to hurt you. I plan to give you hope and a good future."

NOTES

NOTES

DAY 6
TRUSTING GOD'S TIMING

Sometimes, God takes His time.

I'm married. Let me preface this entire devotion by saying that my wife, Casey, is the best thing that has ever happened to me. With that being said, she's not a stickler for time management. Because of her struggle, I know what it's like to know the event's start time, the time we need to leave to arrive on time, and what it feels like when you suddenly realize that you never were going to make it on time.

Here's the reality: before the panic begins, before I start to rush Casey, and before the clock continuously ticks, I already know there's a possibility that we'll be late, yet I remain hopeful. I panic, pace back and forth, and try to convince my wife to speed up, which only slows her down. All the while, Casey is calm, cool, and collected, as if we're early.

This seems very similar to our relationship with God. I symbolize us as God's children, and Casey symbolizes God. The same way I panic and try to rush Casey is the same way we panic and try to rush God. But, in these moments, we must try to embrace the truth that His timing is beyond our comprehension and His timing is always perfect.

We must embrace the paradox that sometimes God takes His time, but even when He takes His time, He's still on time. Don't allow the wait to take your hope. Don't allow the wait to take your peace. Use the wait to draw closer to Him.

Once I have discovered that we're late, I go and crank the car, get all the girls fastened in their seatbelts, find the music we're going to listen to, put the address in the GPS, and soon after, Casey comes out. Once I stop waiting, Casey appears.

So maybe we should stop waiting and start worshiping. Stop waiting and start praying. Stop waiting and start studying. And when God shows up, we won't even realize we are still waiting.

Isaiah 55:8-9 ERV
"8 The Lord says, "My thoughts are not like yours. Your ways are not like mine. 9 Just as the heavens are higher than the earth, so my ways are higher than your ways, and my thoughts are higher than your thoughts."

Romans 12:12 ERV
"12 Be happy because of the hope you have. Be patient when you have troubles. Pray all the time."

NOTES

NOTES

DAY 7
TRANSITIONING WITHIN

Transition starts internally before manifesting externally.

Have you ever just felt off? What was once fulfilling just isn't as fulfilling anymore. Days get longer while your patience rapidly shrinks. This typically means some type of change or evolution is happening.

Now, I'm not suggesting that when these feelings occur, it means it's time to abort, jump ship, and burn bridges, but I do think these feelings are worth investigating.

Often, transition starts before it's seen. There's an internal work that God begins in us when He's directing us toward a shift. It's His way of preparing you before placing you. Don't ignore God's transition hints. Don't ignore the subtle changes in your thinking, behaviors, speech, and/or relationships.

Take the time to investigate if it is God-initiated. Take the time to understand what you're feeling and why you're feeling it. Truly reflect on when these emotions began and what may have triggered them. Gauge with those closest to you to see if they have noticed the difference in you. Most importantly, search the scriptures for what you're feeling.

Investigating these feelings is in your best interest because God often goes silent during this phase of transition. Yep. In a season where you need Him the most because of all the changes you feel, it almost seems impossible to get a clear answer from Him.

That's because although transition is God-initiated, transition has to be personally navigated.

In most cases, God's not in the business of dragging you to your next. Instead, He offers an invitation to new possibilities.

Will you accept His invitation?

Revelation 3:20 ERV
"20 Here I am! I stand at the door and knock. If you hear my voice and open the door, I will come in and eat with you. And you will eat with me."

2 Corinthians 5:17 ERV
"17 When anyone is in Christ, it is a whole new world. The old things are gone; suddenly, everything is new!"

NOTES

NOTES

DAY 8
TRANSITIONING OUT

Remember, this is an exit, but it's also an entrance.

Exits are rarely easy. Whether you are exiting a job, relationship, friendship, or opportunity, it can be tough, especially if you've invested your time, talent, and treasure. Walking away often begins a grieving process, even if better is on the horizon.

That's why it is important to allow grief to run its course. *Feel your feelings when you feel them. Otherwise, they will make you feel them at the most inopportune time*.

Often, we can dismiss our emotions as if they don't exist for a legitimate reason. Trust me, those emotions are more legitimate than you give them credit for. Exits can be painful, stressful, and exhausting because exiting is a choice to leave all that is familiar. And as we stated on Day Two, whether we realize it or not, familiarity is something most of our hearts seek.

Abandoning comfort is a direct contradiction to our natural desire to be comfortable. It can sometimes put our spirit and our heart at war because saying yes in the spirit doesn't mean your heart agrees. Allowing yourself to grieve while seeking God's direction can put your spirit and your heart back in alignment.

Whatever the reason for your exit, remember to exit carefully. One season ending doesn't mean you'll never return to the people or place you left. Be careful not to burn bridges on your way out.

You never know if you'll need to cross that bridge again to get to what God has for you.

This life has become more about who you know than what you know. Be intentional about loving and respecting people on your way out so that they won't be a hindrance on your way up.

Psalm 121:8 ERV
"8 The Lord will protect you as you come and go, both now and forever!"

Deuteronomy 28:2-6 NIV
"2 All these blessings will come on you and accompany you if you obey the Lord your God: 3 You will be blessed in the city and blessed in the country. 4 The fruit of your womb will be blessed, and the crops of your land and the young of your livestock—the calves of your herds and the lambs of your flocks. 5 Your basket and your kneading trough will be blessed. 6 You will be blessed when you come in and blessed when you go out"

NOTES

NOTES

DAY 9
TRANSITIONING FROM PEOPLE

It's hard to transition from people.

Transition comes in all forms, shapes, and sizes, but transitioning from people is one of the hardest transitions to navigate. Having people in your life is essential for emotional well-being, personal development, and overall life satisfaction.

If we correctly assess people's importance in our lives, we'll realize the true value of relationships. Think about it. A house becomes a home because of people. A congregation becomes a family because of people. A job becomes a joy because of people. Without people, a cookout just becomes burnt food. College is just targeted instruction without people. Our best experiences as customers most likely happened because of people. As much as they get on our nerves and as much as we want a break from people, the reality is we need people.

After all, we were designed to thrive in community rather than isolation. In Genesis, while Adam is working in the garden alone, God even realizes that man needs help. That's why when you find good people, you try to hold on and never let go. And that's also why when we're familiar with unhealthy people, we'll stick around although they're not good for us.

It's hard to transition from people. Here's what I've learned over the years: some people are in your life for the rest of your life, regardless of where you are and regardless of where they are. Other people are in your life for a season, occupying a space for a certain time.

It's a hard pill to swallow, especially when we think that seasonal friendships are lifetime friendships.

The best way to transition from people is to get ahead of it even if they don't understand it. If you know transition is on the horizon, share it with those in your life so they can process it in their own way. That's what Jesus did. When He was preparing to sacrifice Himself by dying on the cross for our sins, Jesus told his disciples what He knew was coming. His disclosure brought some in closer, like John, in whom Jesus felt confident enough to protect and cover His mother after His death. On the other hand, Jesus's news pushed some away, like Judas, who sold Jesus out for 30 pieces of silver. Transition will show you who is with you for life and who is with you for a season.

Genesis 2:18 ERV
"18 Then the Lord God said, "I see that it is not good for the man to be alone. I will make the companion he needs, one just right for him.""

Matthew 16:21 ERV
"21 From that time on Jesus began to explain to his disciples that he must go to Jerusalem and suffer many things at the hands of the elders, the chief priests, and the teachers of the law, and that he must be killed and on the third day be raised to life.""

Joshua 1:9 ERV
"9 Remember, I commanded you to be strong and brave. Don't be afraid, because the Lord your God will be with you wherever you go.""

NOTES

NOTES

DAY 10
TRANSITIONING FROM PLACES

Transitioning from a place is a process.

One of the most common transitions that people navigate at some point is from places. Although it's common, it's not the easiest to navigate. Certain places hold a unique power and influence over our lives, shaping our experiences, memories, and even our identity. Think about how much your church has shaped you over the years. What about your childhood home? How about your Elementary school, Middle school, or High school? Places where significant life events occur carry emotional weight and are hard to escape even when necessary. Somehow, these places become more than just geographical locations; they become receptacles of emotions, culture, and history for us.

Transitioning from places can be expected or unexpected, joyous or depressing, voluntary or mandatory. We move out of places, graduate from places, outgrow places, and the list goes on. Regardless of how the transition is initiated and what state we're in when we transition, transitioning from a place is still a process. There are a range of emotions that you'll feel. There is a list of accomplishments and regrets that will run through your mind. It's a process that you can't escape. Escaping a place doesn't mean you can escape the process.

Because the places in our lives are more than locations, we have to be careful to manage our exits properly. Managing exits from places properly requires thoughtful consideration and emotional intelligence. Take time to reflect on the significance of that place and acknowledge the experiences, relationships, and personal growth that occurred.

Show appreciation for the people and experiences that made that place important to you. Consider the skills, knowledge, and personal insights you gained there. Believe in your heart that there is no such thing as wasted experiences. You can learn from every place you've been planted. And remember, managing exits is not only about closing a chapter but also leveraging the experience gained to embark on a new journey.

The most important way to manage your exits from places properly is to know that God is with you. In Exodus 3, when God instructed Moses to lead the entire nation of Israel out of Egypt, Moses was overwhelmed and uncertain if he had what it took to complete this task. God's promise to Moses was the assurance that Moses needed. "You can do it because I will be with you."

Exodus 3:7-12 ERV
"7 Then the Lord said, "I have seen the troubles my people have suffered in Egypt, and I have heard their cries when the Egyptians hurt them. I know about their pain. 8 Now I will go down and save my people from the Egyptians. I will take them from that land and lead them to a good land where they can be free from these troubles. It is a land filled with many good things. Many different people live in that land: the Canaanites, Hittites, Amorites, Perizzites, Hivites, and Jebusites. 9 I have heard the cries of the Israelites, and I have seen the way the Egyptians have made life hard for them. 10 So now I am sending you to Pharaoh. Go! Lead my people, the Israelites, out of Egypt." 11 But Moses said to God, "I am not a great man! How can I be the one to go to Pharaoh and lead the Israelites out of Egypt?" 12 God said, "You can do it because I will be with you.""

NOTES

NOTES

DAY 11
TRANSITIONING FROM PATTERNS

Patterns become a natural part of who we are and what we do.

Patterns or habits, whether good or bad, are hard to break. We all know a bad habit when we see one, right? And in most cases, we can pinpoint or recognize when a bad habit needs to be broken. This is because bad habits typically become visible over time. They are hard to break because, at some point, they become a natural part of who we are and what we do. Sometimes, we knowingly continue bad habits because it is more natural for us to engage in them rather than live without them. But bad habits are not the only habits that require transition. Sometimes, we also have to break away from healthy habits.

Healthy habits play an extremely significant role in our lives, offering efficiency, structure, and positive behaviors. Healthy habits are typically not our issue until they begin to control us. Even healthy habits can be harmful when they create dependency on them rather than dependence on God. If healthy habits are not monitored, they can shift from efficiency to rigidity, structure to unconscious behavior, and from positive behavior to robotic behavior without us even knowing it.

Creating healthy habits is extremely important, but maintaining the health of the habit is more important. It is similar to the maintenance of a yard. Nothing sticks out more in a yard than weeds. But weeds do not start as the weeds we pull; they start as seeds we do not notice. There are various ways these seeds can be introduced: some are carried by the wind, birds and animals carry some, some are attached to shoes and clothing, some come from rainfall, and some come from garden waste.

Regardless of how the seeds appear, they all germinate and grow quickly into weeds that choke the life out of the positive aspect of your landscape.

If your yard isn't properly maintained, it will be destroyed by the weeds you allow to grow. Bad habits and expired habits are like weeds. They cannot just be cut; they must be pulled from the root; otherwise, they will return.

Romans 12:2 ERV
"2 Don't change yourselves to be like the people of this world, but let God change you inside with a new way of thinking. Then you will be able to understand and accept what God wants for you. You will be able to know what is good and pleasing to him and what is perfect."

NOTES

NOTES

DAY 12
IN BETWEEN TRANSITIONS

In-between seasons create space for the miraculous.

Being stuck in between transitions is the worst! But is it really? It can be extremely frustrating to be stuck in a cycle of "no longer" and "not yet" all at the same time. You are no longer where you were, but you aren't yet where you are going, so you have to survive the in-between.

The in-between can be a tricky place. It has the power to make you feel like you have missed your moment. It has the power to make you feel like you did not hear God correctly. It also has the power to make you question whether or not your leap of faith was worth it. The in-between creates an illusion that God didn't say what He did say and that God isn't going to do what He will do. You have to be careful in the in-between and recognize that there is purpose in the in-between.

In-between seasons offer a unique beauty. It's a time of subtle transformation, a pause between extremes, allowing for reflection and anticipation for what's to come. There's a chance for growth in the in-between, where you can learn valuable lessons about yourself that lead to profound self-discovery. In-between seasons teach us the art of embracing the unpredictable, where we encounter unexpected opportunities that spark creativity, leading to new ideas and innovative approaches.

The most important purpose of in-between seasons may be creating space for the miraculous. When you are between a closed door and an open door, you become open to the unlimited power of God's provision and protection. You have full reliance on His ability and not your own. You are in a vulnerable state of "if God doesn't do it, it won't be done." And sometimes, that is the best place for us to be.

Lastly, in-between seasons make us appreciate "walk-into" seasons much more. You walk into your next guarded with pride and arrogance when you do not serve time in the in-between. When you walk into your next after being stuck in between, you walk in it with a heart of gratitude because you understand that God did not have to open the door for you.

Navigating in-between seasons is similar to a caterpillar waiting in its cocoon. It takes a season of patience and resilience, but somehow, transformation takes place while you're waiting. On the other side of the wait is a masterpiece of beauty.

Psalm 27:14 ERV
"14 Wait for the Lord's help. Be strong and brave, and wait for the Lord's help."

Lamentations 3:25-26 ERV
"25 The Lord is good to those who wait for him. He is good to those who look for him. 26 It is good to wait quietly for the Lord to save them."

2 Corinthians 4:16-18 ERV
"16 That is why we never give up. Our physical body is becoming older and weaker, but the spirit inside us is made new every day. 17 We have had small troubles for a while now, but these troubles are helping us gain an eternal glory. That eternal glory is much greater than our troubles. 18 So we think about what we cannot see, not what we see. What we see lasts only a short time, and what we cannot see will last forever."

NOTES

NOTES

-

DAY 13
TRANSITIONING IN

Beware of the danger of misplaced punishment.

Have you ever had a really bad day? Traffic is bad. On your way to work, every light is red, and you're already late. You get to work, and your co-workers get on your nerves. Your boss throws more at you as if you're not already drowning in assignments. Bills are due. Problems continue to arise throughout the day, but you carry all that weight gracefully. Then you get home to the people you love, and they get the worst of you when they aren't the cause of any of your issues.

That's how a lot of us transition into our next. Our next hasn't caused any of our frustrations, yet we walk in with our guard up. We're hesitant to put ourselves out there and unwilling to accept that it is as good as it seems. Be careful with that. Don't punish your new because of your old's crimes. Give your new and give God a fair chance to meet and/or exceed your expectations.

Transition in with confidence that God brought you here.
Transition in with assurance that this is the Lord's doing.
Transition in with faith that things will work out.
Transition in with the hope that this is for the best.
Transition in with the expectation that better days are ahead.

Do not walk into your new with old expectations, perceptions, habits, and mindsets. Do not resist the change you've already committed to. Embrace what your new has to offer.

And yes. You're right. It's not the same. But it was never intended to be. You did not make the choice, you did not transition within, and you did not transition out for things to remain the same. You read Days 1-12 of this devotional because you were embracing change. Do not abandon it now.

Now, is it possible that the new will end just like the old? Absolutely! This could turn out to be the worst experience ever. But the new could also be the best thing that ever happens to you. Don't forfeit that possibility before the game begins.

Isaiah 43:18-19 ERV
"18 So don't remember what happened in earlier times. Don't think about what happened a long time ago, 19 because I am doing something new! Now you will grow like a new plant. Surely you know this is true. I will even make a road in the desert, and rivers will flow through that dry land."

Luke 5:37-38 ERV
"37 Also, no one ever pours new wine into old wineskins. The new wine would break them. The wine would spill out, and the wineskins would be ruined. 38 You always put new wine into new wineskins."

Psalm 118: 23-24 ERV
"23 The Lord made this happen, and we think it is wonderful! 24 This is the day the Lord has made. Let us rejoice and be happy today!"

NOTES

NOTES

DAY 14
NOW, GIVE IT SOME TIME

Time will show you everything you need to know.

Your transition needs time. It is a rare instance where everything immediately feels perfect, and when those rare instances occur, you still need time. You do not want all of your faith to crumble from one bad moment, nor do you want to get caught up in a facade of emotions. Trust me, time is your friend.

Often, we treat time like an ugly friend we do not like to be seen with, but time is much cuter than you think; it may not be cute in the face, but it has some beautiful aspects that we should not overlook.

The best attribute of time is that it will show you everything you need to know. Time will show you everything you need to know about people, places, positions, patterns, systems, relationships, and yourself. Allowing new transitions time to work is crucial because meaningful changes often require adaptation and adjustment.

Never be fooled by time, thinking it is a waste of time. Time offers us so much without us even realizing it. It offers:

  - **Moments of Serendipity**: If you allow it to, time unfolds unexpected moments of joy, connection, and discovery.
  - **Personal Growth**: Over time, you can learn, evolve, grow, and acquire wisdom and experience.

- **Nostalgia**: Time allows for creating memories, reminding us of meaningful moments.
- **Creativity and Innovation**: Time fosters progress, enabling the development of new ideas, artistic expressions, dreams, gifts, goals, and visions.
- **Relationships**: Time is the canvas on which relationships are painted, built, and strengthened.

One more thing to always remember about time is that it is not capable of keeping a secret. Time will tell you if this transition was initiated by God or something else. Time will tell you if you are supposed to stay or leave. Time will tell you if they are who they claimed they'd be. Time will tell you if this is going to be a purposeful experience or a painful one. If you have transitioned by faith, give it some time.

Ecclesiastes 3:1-8 ERV
"1 There is a right time for everything, and everything on earth will happen at the right time. 2 There is a time to be born and a time to die. There is a time to plant and a time to pull up plants. 3 There is a time to kill and a time to heal. There is a time to destroy and a time to build. 4 There is a time to cry and a time to laugh. There is a time to be sad and a time to dance with joy. 5 There is a time to throw weapons down and a time to pick them up. There is a time to hug someone and a time to stop holding so tightly. 6 There is a time to look for something and a time to consider it lost. There is a time to keep things and a time to throw things away. 7 There is a time to tear cloth and a time to sew it. There is a time to be silent and a time to speak. 8 There is a time to love and a time to hate. There is a time for war and a time for peace."

NOTES

NOTES

TRUSTING THROUGH TRANSITION

I hope this devotional was helpful for you and your journey. As we close, I'd like to pray for you:

Father, first and foremost, we thank You. We thank You for Your goodness and Your direction. We know that You want what's best for us. We also know that You desire to pull the best out of us. We acknowledge that You know where and when the best can take place for us; therefore, Father, we release our control and give You total control.

Father, I pray for my brother and my sister right now. If they are reading this, they are either anticipating transition, in transition, or coming out of transition. Wherever they may be in their journey, send Your Spirit now. Give them a sense of peace that doesn't require understanding. Give them a sense of joy not predicated on people, positions, location, or circumstance. Give them strength that's made perfect in their weakness.

As Your children, we have an advantage because You know our beginning and our end. So lead us, Father. Guide us now. Order our steps, clear our path, and open the double doors of peace, fulfillment, and success.

We vow to trust You. Although we don't have all of the answers, we have You. And that's enough.

In Jesus Name. Amen.

-JT

www.ingramcontent.com/pod-product-compliance
Lightning Source LLC
Chambersburg PA
CBHW051242120626
46547CB00014B/1761